I Can an App

Katie Smythe

Rosen
REAL
READERS

Rosen
Classroom™
New York

I can use an app. I use apps every day on my tablet. Apps help me do different things. I use a **calendar** app to help me keep track of schoolwork.

I can use an app to read books. I can find books to help me write a paper for school. I can read books for fun, too.

I can use an app to draw. The app lets me choose any color I like. I like to draw flowers. Drawing on my **tablet** is fun.

I can use an app to do math. Some apps let me practice math. Some apps have math games. Other apps have math problems.

I can use an app to play a game. Some game apps help me with schoolwork. Some game apps are just for fun. I touch the picture of the game I want to play. The picture is called an **icon**.

I can use an app to play my favorite game. I touch the screen to make my character move around. I practice my reading as I read the directions.

I can use an app to talk with my aunt.

I can hear her voice and see her face.

Now I can see my aunt every day.

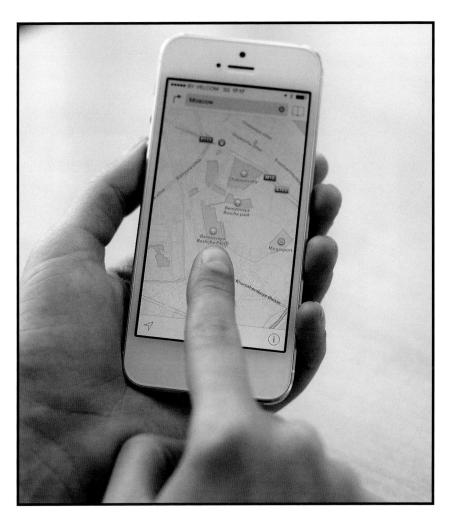

I can use an app to learn about the city where my friend moved. Map apps can help you find a new street. You can also explore a place that is far away.

I can use an app to take a picture. I can use an app to take a **video**. Sometimes my mom and dad use the app to take a video of me!

I can use apps in school. I can learn
math and science with apps. I can share
what I learn with my classmates.

Glossary

calendar   A chart that shows the days, weeks, and months of a year.

icon   A picture that stands for something or tells you what something is.

tablet   A handheld computer that does not have a keyboard or a mouse.

video   A recording of moving visual images.